I0698646

APPLE VISION PRO FEATURES UNVEILED:
All you need to know.

Navigating through The Apple Vision Pro Chronicle and the Future of Personal Computing with Vision Verse.

Arnold Harper

All rights reserved © Arnold Harper
2023

Table of contents

INTRODUCTION

The Evolution of Personal Computing

The journey of personal computing has been nothing short of a technological odyssey. From the humble beginnings of clunky machines with limited capabilities to the sleek, powerful devices we use today, the evolution has been marked by continuous innovation and a quest for a more immersive user experience. It all started with the advent of the personal computer in the late 20th century, a device that initially catered to enthusiasts and businesses but eventually found its way into households, fundamentally changing the way people work, communicate, and entertain themselves.

The initial personal computers, characterized by their monochrome displays and command-line interfaces, laid the foundation for what was to come. The graphical user interface (GUI) revolutionized the user experience, making computing more accessible to the general public. The introduction of iconic products like the Macintosh in 1984 showcased the potential of intuitive interfaces and set the stage for Apple's commitment to user-centric design.

Over the years, personal computing witnessed significant milestones, from the proliferation of laptops to the rise of smartphones and tablets. Each advancement brought new possibilities, transforming computing from a stationary activity to something seamlessly integrated into our daily lives. The evolution continued with the exploration of virtual and augmented reality, pushing the boundaries of how we perceive and interact with digital information.

The Birth of Apple Vision Pro

In the ever-changing landscape of technology, Apple has been a consistent pioneer, known for redefining industries and setting new standards. The birth of Apple Vision Pro represents a culmination of years of research, innovation, and a commitment to pushing the boundaries of what's possible in personal computing.

The idea of a mixed reality headset was not conceived in isolation but as a response to a growing demand for more immersive computing experiences. Apple, with its legacy of groundbreaking products, embarked on a journey to create a device that goes beyond the confines of traditional screens, promising a future where the digital and physical worlds seamlessly merge.

The Vision Pro project didn't just start with the goal of creating another accessory; it aimed to introduce a paradigm shift in how we perceive and engage with digital content. The project was shrouded in secrecy, with speculation and anticipation building in the tech community. As leaks and rumors surfaced, the excitement grew, fueling expectations of a device that would redefine personal computing once again.

The dual-chip architecture of the M2 and R1 processors, a core element of the Vision Pro, was designed to deliver unparalleled performance. This wasn't just about upgrading processing power; it was about creating an environment where lag is virtually eliminated, ensuring a smooth and responsive user experience. The integration of 12 cameras and LiDAR scanners for precise tracking showcased Apple's commitment to creating a device that understands and responds to user movements with meticulous accuracy.

The adaptation of familiar iOS and iPadOS apps to the Vision Pro interface marked a strategic move. It not only provided users with instant access to a vast library of software but also ensured a seamless transition for those already entrenched in the Apple ecosystem. This approach was a testament to Apple's understanding of its user base and the importance of a cohesive user experience across its product lineup.

The Vision Pro wasn't just about utility; it aimed to transform how we capture and relive memories. The advanced cameras, capable of capturing moments in stunning 3D, promised to take users on a journey back in time, immersing them in the sights and sounds of their most cherished experiences. The concept of viewing existing photos and videos at a life-size scale, with panoramas wrapping around users, added a layer of nostalgia and emotion to the device.

Connection, a fundamental aspect of personal computing, was reimagined with the Vision Pro. FaceTime, a staple in Apple's ecosystem, underwent a transformation that made video calls more immersive than ever. Life-size video tiles floating in virtual space made it feel like users were physically present with their loved ones, enhancing the sense of connection. The addition of Spatial Audio, with voices seemingly originating from their respective positions in the virtual space, further blurred the lines between the physical and digital realms.

As we delve deeper into the technical specifications, applications across industries, and the comparisons with other mixed reality headsets in subsequent chapters, it becomes evident that Apple Vision Pro is not just a headset; it's a doorway to a new dimension of computing, offering limitless possibilities. The launch on February 2nd is not just a product release; it's an invitation to step into the future and embrace the transformative power of mixed reality.

CHAPTER ONE

A Paradigm Shift in Computing: Moving Beyond Flat Screens

For decades, personal computing has been synonymous with flat screens—monitors that display two-dimensional representations of our digital world. However, the introduction of Apple Vision Pro heralds a paradigm shift, propelling us beyond the confines of traditional displays into a realm where the digital and physical seamlessly converge. It's a departure from the flatness that has defined our digital experiences, inviting users to explore an immersive three-dimensional space.

The transition from flat screens to mixed reality is not just a change in form; it's a transformation in how we interact with information. With Vision Pro, information is no longer confined to rectangular windows on a screen. Instead, it becomes an integral part of our environment, projected directly onto our field of vision. Whether it's navigating through applications or interacting with digital content, the transition from a flat, two-dimensional interface to a spatial, three-dimensional canvas opens up new possibilities for creativity and productivity.

The shift is not merely cosmetic. It's about breaking free from the limitations of a screen-bound existence. Vision Pro liberates our digital experiences, allowing us to arrange apps in three-dimensional space at any scale. This not only enhances multitasking but also fundamentally changes how we organize and engage with our digital workspace. The traditional desktop metaphor gives way to an infinite canvas, where the spatial arrangement of applications reflects a more intuitive and dynamic workflow.

The Concept of Mixed Reality

At the heart of this paradigm shift is the concept of mixed reality (MR), a blend of both augmented reality (AR) and virtual reality (VR). While AR overlays digital content onto the real world, VR immerses users entirely in a simulated environment. Apple Vision Pro seamlessly combines these elements, creating a cohesive mixed reality experience that goes beyond what we've seen before.

In the MR space, Vision Pro transcends the limitations of AR and VR as standalone technologies. It doesn't just augment the world around you; it transforms it entirely, creating a harmonious interplay between the physical and digital realms. This dynamic fusion opens up unprecedented opportunities for innovative applications, from productivity tools to entertainment experiences that bridge the gap between reality and imagination.

The Vision Pro's approach to mixed reality is not about escapism; it's about enhancing our everyday interactions with technology. Imagine your favorite applications appearing in 3D around you, not confined to a screen but existing as dynamic elements in your physical space. This immersive integration of the digital into our daily lives blurs the boundaries between what's real and what's virtual, creating a rich and engaging user experience.

Dual-Chip Architecture: M2 and R1 Processors

Central to the transformative capabilities of Apple Vision Pro is its powerhouse within – the dual-chip architecture featuring the M2 and R1 processors. This combination represents a significant leap in processing power and efficiency, setting the stage for a mixed reality experience that's not only visually stunning but also remarkably responsive.

The M2 processor, known for its prowess in Apple's lineup, handles the general computing tasks, ensuring a smooth and seamless operation of applications. Its efficiency is crucial in providing a lag-free environment, a vital aspect of mixed reality where real-time responsiveness is paramount. The M2's capabilities extend beyond traditional computing demands, optimized to deliver a performance that meets the unique requirements of mixed reality interactions.

Complementing the M2 is the R1 processor, dedicated specifically to the demands of mixed reality experiences. This specialized chip tackles the complex task of rendering 3D environments and managing the intricate spatial tracking system. The result is a headset that not only keeps up with the user's movements but does so with meticulous precision, creating an immersive experience free from the disorienting lag often associated with virtual and augmented reality devices.

The seamless collaboration between the M2 and R1 processors exemplifies Apple's commitment to pushing the boundaries of what's possible in personal computing. It's not just about raw power; it's about a finely tuned orchestration of hardware, working in harmony to deliver an experience that defines the next era of computing.

As we delve deeper into the technical intricacies of the dual-chip architecture, exploring its impact on performance and user experience, it becomes clear that the M2 and R1 processors are the driving force behind the paradigm shift Apple Vision Pro brings to the world of computing. The transition from flat screens to mixed reality is not just a visual upgrade; it's a fundamental reimagining of how we engage with digital information, and at its core lies the transformative power of advanced, purpose-built processors.

CHAPTER TWO

Spatial Computing Breakthrough: Projecting onto Your Field of Vision

The spatial computing breakthrough brought forth by Apple Vision Pro represents a monumental leap in the way we interact with digital content. No longer confined to the limitations of flat screens, Vision Pro projects information and applications directly onto your field of vision, transforming the way we perceive and engage with the digital world.

Imagine a scenario where your digital workspace is not confined to the physical boundaries of a screen but exists in the three-dimensional space around you. With spatial computing, this vision becomes a reality. Applications and information aren't limited to rectangular windows; they float in the air, seamlessly integrated into your surroundings. This spatial projection not only enhances the visual appeal but fundamentally changes the way we navigate and interact with digital content.

The projection isn't arbitrary; it's a dynamic response to your movements and gestures. As you look around or reach out, the digital elements adjust in real-time, creating an immersive experience that feels intuitive and natural. This seamless integration of the digital into our physical environment opens up new possibilities for productivity, creativity, and entertainment.

The Power of M2 and R1: Lag Elimination

Key to the success of spatial computing is the elimination of lag, ensuring that the digital elements respond instantaneously to user actions. This is precisely where the power of the M2 and R1 processors comes into play. The M2 processor, known for its general computing prowess, collaborates with the R1 processor, dedicated specifically to mixed reality experiences, to deliver a performance that sets a new standard in responsiveness.

Lag has long been a challenge in virtual and augmented reality environments, often causing discomfort and disorientation. The dual-chip architecture of the Vision Pro addresses this challenge head-on. The M2 processor handles the general computing tasks, ensuring a smooth operation of applications, while the R1 processor takes charge of rendering 3D environments and managing spatial tracking. The synergy between these processors virtually eliminates lag, creating an experience that feels not just seamless but natural.

The absence of lag is not just about comfort; it's about the effectiveness of spatial computing. Whether you're navigating through a virtual environment, interacting with 3D models, or enjoying an immersive entertainment experience, the responsiveness of Vision Pro ensures that the digital elements move and react as if they are part of the physical world. This lag elimination sets a new standard for mixed reality devices, making Vision Pro a pioneer in providing a truly immersive and user-friendly experience.

Precision Tracking: 12 Cameras and LiDAR Scanners

Spatial computing requires a high degree of precision in tracking user movements and gestures. Apple Vision Pro achieves this with a sophisticated system of 12 cameras and LiDAR scanners. These sensors work in unison to track the position and orientation of the headset, ensuring that the digital elements align seamlessly with the user's real-world environment.

The 12 cameras, strategically positioned around the Vision Pro headset, capture a comprehensive view of the surroundings. This multi-camera setup enables accurate depth perception and allows the device to understand the user's position in relation to the digital content. As the user moves, the cameras track every nuance, translating these movements into real-time adjustments in the digital projection.

LiDAR (Light Detection and Ranging) scanners add another layer of precision to the tracking system. By emitting laser beams and measuring the time it takes for them to bounce back, LiDAR creates a detailed, real-time map of the surroundings. This technology is particularly effective in low-light conditions, enhancing the overall tracking accuracy of Vision Pro.

The combination of cameras and LiDAR scanners creates a meticulous tracking system that not only responds to large movements but also captures subtle gestures. Whether you're reaching out to interact with a virtual object or simply turning your head to explore a 3D environment, the precision tracking ensures that the digital elements align with your movements seamlessly.

This level of precision is not just a technological feat; it's a critical component in delivering a natural and immersive mixed reality experience. It allows users to interact with digital content in a way that feels instinctive, bridging the gap between the physical and digital realms. As we delve into the technical intricacies of the spatial computing breakthrough, it becomes clear that Apple Vision Pro is not just a device; it's a meticulously engineered system that redefines how we perceive and interact with the digital world.

CHAPTER THREE

Apps Reimagined

The introduction of Apple Vision Pro brings a revolutionary concept to the forefront: the infinite canvas for apps. No longer confined to the limitations of flat screens, apps on Vision Pro have the freedom to exist in a three-dimensional space, offering users a dynamic and immersive way to interact with their digital tools.

Picture a workspace where your applications are not bound by the rectangular constraints of a traditional display. Instead, they float around you, each one existing as a distinct entity in the spatial environment. This concept transforms the traditional desktop metaphor into a boundless canvas, where users can arrange and organize apps in a way that mirrors how they think and work.

The infinite canvas is not merely a cosmetic enhancement; it redefines how users approach productivity and creativity. It allows for a more intuitive and spatially aware organization of digital tools. Whether you're working on a complex project, arranging design elements, or simply managing your day-to-day tasks, the infinite canvas provides a versatile and fluid environment that adapts to your needs.

This shift in app design is a departure from the static nature of traditional interfaces. Instead of opening and closing windows, users can position apps around them, creating a visual and interactive landscape that mirrors the way they conceptualize their work. The infinite canvas concept is not just a feature; it's a fundamental reimagining of how we engage with our digital tools, ushering in a new era of spatial computing.

Multitasking in 3D

Multitasking takes on a new dimension with Apple Vision Pro, quite literally. The ability to work on multiple tasks simultaneously is redefined in a three-dimensional space, introducing a level of flexibility and efficiency that goes beyond what we've experienced with traditional computing.

In a traditional multitasking environment, users switch between open applications or view them side by side on a flat screen. Vision Pro takes this concept to the next level by allowing users to arrange and interact with multiple apps in 3D space. Imagine drafting an email while having a 3D model or document open in the same virtual environment. The spatial organization not only enhances multitasking capabilities but also facilitates a more natural and fluid workflow.

The three-dimensional nature of multitasking on Vision Pro mirrors how our minds naturally handle multiple tasks. Users can position apps at different distances and angles, creating a visual hierarchy that reflects the priority and relationship between tasks. This spatial organization is not just a visual enhancement but a functional one, as it provides users with a more intuitive way to manage and navigate their digital workspace.

The concept of multitasking in 3D extends beyond productivity. It transforms the way users consume content, play games, or engage in creative endeavors. Watching a video while browsing through related content, designing in a virtual space while referencing inspiration – these scenarios showcase the versatility and depth that 3D multitasking brings to the user experience.

Adapting iOS and iPadOS Apps to Vision Pro

With the launch of Apple Vision Pro, users can seamlessly transition into the mixed reality experience with their favorite iOS and iPadOS apps. This adaptation is not just about compatibility; it's about reimagining how these apps can thrive in a three-dimensional environment, opening up a world of possibilities for users familiar with the Apple ecosystem.

The process of adapting iOS and iPadOS apps to Vision Pro involves more than a straightforward port. It's about optimizing the user interface and interaction models to align with the spatial computing paradigm. Apps are no longer confined to the flat surfaces of screens; they become dynamic elements that users can position and interact with in a 3D space.

Familiarity is a key aspect of this adaptation. Users accustomed to the iOS and iPadOS interfaces will find a seamless transition as their favorite apps retain their core functionality. However, the spatial adaptation introduces a new layer of engagement. Whether it's navigating through a 3D representation of your calendar, exploring a spatially organized file system, or interacting with social media in a more immersive way, the adaptation ensures that the essence of each app is enhanced rather than compromised.

This compatibility doesn't just benefit users; it opens up a world of opportunities for developers. The growing ecosystem of Vision Pro developers is actively exploring ways to leverage the device's spatial computing capabilities. This includes not only adapting existing apps but also creating new and innovative experiences that harness the full potential of mixed reality.

As we delve into the reimagined landscape of apps on Vision Pro, it becomes clear that this is not just an incremental upgrade; it's a transformative shift in how we perceive and interact with digital applications. The infinite canvas, 3D multitasking, and the seamless adaptation of iOS and iPadOS apps collectively create an ecosystem where digital tools become dynamic extensions of our thoughts and actions, defining a new standard in spatial computing.

CHAPTER FOUR

Memories Transformed

Advanced Cameras for 3D Capture

Apple Vision Pro doesn't just redefine how we interact with the digital world; it revolutionizes how we capture and relive our most cherished memories. At the heart of this transformative experience are the advanced cameras designed explicitly for 3D capture. These cameras are not mere lenses but sophisticated tools that enable users to capture moments in a way that transcends traditional photography and videography.

The 3D capture capability of Vision Pro's cameras introduces a new dimension to memory preservation. Instead of capturing a flat representation of a scene, these cameras create a spatial map that retains the depth and dimensionality of the environment. Imagine taking a photo of a family gathering or a scenic landscape and being able to revisit that moment with an unprecedented level of immersion. This is the promise of advanced 3D capture.

The cameras utilize cutting-edge technology to precisely capture the geometry and texture of the subjects. Whether it's people, objects, or environments, the result is a rich and detailed representation that goes beyond what traditional cameras can achieve. This level of detail is not just about visual fidelity; it's about creating a true-to-life experience when revisiting these memories in mixed reality.

Reliving Moments in Spatial Detail

The true magic of Vision Pro's advanced cameras unfolds when users revisit these captured moments in spatial detail. Instead of flipping through static photos or watching flat videos, users can immerse themselves in the scene, experiencing the sights and sounds as if transported back in time.

Spatial detail goes beyond conventional photography or videography. It's about capturing the essence of a moment in its entirety. When reliving a captured memory, users can explore the spatial nuances – the way light played on surfaces, the spatial arrangement of people and objects, and even the ambient sounds that accompanied the scene. It's a level of immersion that brings memories to life in a way previously unimaginable.

This spatial detail is particularly impactful when applied to significant life events. Imagine revisiting a wedding ceremony, a graduation, or a family vacation with a level of detail that makes you feel like you're not just watching a recording but actually stepping back into that moment. The emotional resonance of such an experience is profound, creating a deeper connection to our past.

Moreover, the spatial detail isn't limited to just the moment of capture. Users can interact with these memories in real-time, exploring different angles, perspectives, and even adding elements to enhance the experience. This dynamic interaction with memories elevates the concept of reliving moments, turning it into an active and engaging process.

Life-Size Photo and Video Viewing

The culmination of advanced cameras and spatial detail comes to life in the form of life-size photo and video viewing on Apple Vision Pro. The traditional approach to viewing photos and videos on flat screens is transcended as Vision Pro transforms your space into a canvas where memories come to life in their true scale.

Imagine standing amidst larger-than-life representations of your most cherished photos, the images wrapping around you, creating a panoramic experience that evokes a deep sense of nostalgia. This life-size viewing isn't just about showcasing the visual content; it's about immersing users in the emotional tapestry of their memories.

For videos, the life-size viewing experience adds a cinematic quality to personal moments. Instead of watching on a small screen, users can have a front-row seat to their memories, the spatial audio enhancing the realism as voices and sounds seem to emanate from their corresponding positions in the virtual space.

The life-size viewing concept goes beyond a mere visual spectacle. It aligns with how we naturally perceive and remember events in our lives. When memories are presented in their true scale, the emotional impact is heightened, creating a viewing experience that resonates on a visceral level.

This transformative approach to photo and video viewing is not just a technical feat; it's a testament to the human-centered design philosophy that Apple is renowned for. The goal is not just to present memories in a novel way but to evoke a genuine emotional response, creating an immersive journey through one's own life story.

In conclusion, the "Memories Transformed" aspect of Apple Vision Pro is not just a feature; it's a profound reimagining of how we capture, relive, and interact with the tapestry of our lives. The advanced cameras, coupled with the ability to revisit moments in spatial detail and experience life-size viewing, create a mixed reality album that goes beyond the confines of traditional photo albums and videos. It's a journey through time and space, where memories are not just preserved but truly transformed.

CHAPTER FIVE

Connection Deepened

FaceTime Reinvented

The evolution of personal communication takes a groundbreaking leap with the reinvention of FaceTime on Apple Vision Pro. FaceTime, already a cornerstone of Apple's ecosystem, is not just integrated into the mixed reality experience; it's reimagined to create a sense of connection that transcends geographical distances. This reinvention isn't just about video calls; it's about fostering a feeling of shared presence, as if everyone involved is in the same room.

The standard video call format is transformed as Vision Pro introduces life-size video tiles floating in virtual space. Instead of seeing faces confined to a screen, users experience the sensation of their loved ones physically present around them. The spatial computing capabilities of Vision Pro create a dynamic environment where the size and placement of video tiles mimic the arrangement of people in a physical space.

This spatial arrangement is not just a visual enhancement; it's a psychological one. Human interaction is deeply influenced by spatial cues, and FaceTime on Vision Pro taps into this fundamental aspect of communication. Whether it's a family gathering, a business meeting, or a casual conversation with friends, the spatial arrangement of video tiles creates a sense of togetherness that goes beyond the flatness of traditional video calls.

Moreover, FaceTime on Vision Pro extends beyond the constraints of a single room. Users can move through their physical space, and the spatial audio adapts to the changing perspectives. This dynamic interaction creates a fluid and natural conversation experience, allowing users to engage with their virtual environment while staying connected with others.

Spatial Audio for Immersive Calls

One of the key elements that deepen the connection on Apple Vision Pro is the integration of spatial audio into FaceTime calls. Spatial audio is not merely a feature; it's a transformative technology that enhances the immersion and realism of audio interactions in mixed reality. Instead of hearing voices as flat, monolithic sounds, users experience a nuanced and three-dimensional audio environment.

In a traditional video call, audio is usually presented in a flat, stereo format. However, spatial audio on Vision Pro replicates the natural way we perceive sounds in the physical world. If a person is on your left, their voice will sound like it's coming from the left, creating a sense of directionality that mimics real-life conversations.

This spatial audio extends beyond just left and right; it includes height as well. If someone is speaking from a virtual space above you, their voice will sound as if it's originating from that elevated position. This adds an additional layer of realism to the audio experience, creating a more immersive and engaging conversation.

The integration of spatial audio is particularly impactful in group calls. As multiple participants engage in the conversation, the spatial audio adapts to create a sense of depth and distance between voices. This dynamic audio landscape ensures that users can focus on specific speakers, enhancing the overall clarity and comprehension of the conversation.

In addition to enhancing the realism of FaceTime calls, spatial audio also complements the spatial computing features of Vision Pro. If a user moves within their physical space, the audio adapts accordingly. If someone in the virtual call is on the right, moving to the right in the physical space will make their voice appear louder and more centered. This synchronized audio experience creates a seamless connection between the virtual and physical environments.

Furthermore, the integration of spatial audio extends to other aspects of the mixed reality experience on Vision Pro. Whether users are exploring virtual environments, interacting with 3D content, or enjoying immersive entertainment, spatial audio enriches the overall experience by creating an audio landscape that aligns with the spatial computing paradigm.

In conclusion, the reinvention of FaceTime and the integration of spatial audio on Apple Vision Pro deepen the connection in ways that extend beyond the traditional confines of video calls. It's not just about seeing and hearing; it's about creating a shared sense of space and presence. These features redefine how we connect with others, making virtual interactions on Vision Pro feel more lifelike and emotionally resonant. The combination of life-size video tiles and spatial audio transforms FaceTime from a communication tool into a shared virtual space, fostering a deeper and more immersive connection between individuals separated by physical distances.

CHAPTER SIX

Additional Features

EyeSight Technology: Presence Indicator

Apple Vision Pro introduces a groundbreaking feature that goes beyond the immersive experiences and spatial computing capabilities—EyeSight technology. This innovative addition serves as more than just a technological advancement; it becomes a presence indicator, offering a subtle yet profound way to communicate and enhance the social dynamics of mixed reality interactions.

EyeSight technology leverages advanced sensors to detect and subtly reveal the user's eyes when wearing Vision Pro. This seemingly small detail becomes a powerful element in the realm of mixed reality. In virtual environments where physical presence is simulated, the ability to convey the direction of one's gaze adds a layer of authenticity to the experience. When users look at digital objects or engage with others in the virtual space, their eye movements become a form of non-verbal communication.

The presence indicator not only enhances the realism of social interactions but also addresses a fundamental aspect of human communication—eye contact. In physical interactions, eye contact plays a crucial role in conveying attention, interest, and engagement. EyeSight technology ensures that this vital social cue is not lost in the transition to mixed reality. Whether in a business meeting, a virtual gathering, or a shared experience with friends, the subtle presence of eyes adds a layer of human connection that goes beyond the visual and auditory aspects of communication.

Moreover, EyeSight technology contributes to the overall safety and etiquette in mixed reality environments. By indicating the user's presence, it allows others to know when someone is engaged in the virtual space, preventing potential misunderstandings and enhancing the sense of shared presence. This attention to the social dynamics of mixed reality showcases Apple's commitment to creating not just a technologically advanced device but a platform that respects and enhances human interactions.

Comfortable and Customizable Modular Design

Beyond the technological innovations, Apple Vision Pro places a strong emphasis on comfort and personalization through its customizable modular design. Recognizing that mixed reality experiences can be extended and immersive, the device is crafted to ensure extended use without compromising user comfort.

The modular design allows users to customize the fit and feel of Vision Pro to match their preferences. From adjustable straps to adaptable components, users can tailor the headset to their unique physical characteristics, ensuring a comfortable and secure fit during prolonged usage. The attention to ergonomics is not just a convenience; it's a key factor in promoting the adoption and integration of Vision Pro into various aspects of daily life.

The lightweight and balanced construction of Vision Pro further contribute to the overall comfort. The device is designed to be unobtrusive, allowing users to focus on the mixed reality experiences rather than feeling encumbered by the hardware.

Whether engaged in work, entertainment, or social interactions, the comfort-focused design ensures that users can seamlessly transition between the physical and digital worlds without physical discomfort or distraction.

Additionally, the modular design extends beyond physical comfort to include user preferences in the virtual space. Vision Pro allows users to personalize their mixed reality environment, adjusting elements such as the layout of digital applications, the appearance of avatars, and even the color scheme of the virtual interface. This customization adds a personal touch to the mixed reality experience, creating a platform that adapts to individual preferences and enhances the sense of ownership over the virtual environment.

Furthermore, Apple's commitment to sustainability is evident in the modular design, allowing for easier repairs and upgrades. This not only extends the lifespan of the device but also aligns with the principles of environmental responsibility.

Developer Ecosystem: Pushing Boundaries

Apple Vision Pro is not just a device; it's part of a thriving developer ecosystem that is actively pushing the boundaries of what's possible in mixed reality. The platform invites developers to explore new frontiers, create unique experiences, and redefine the landscape of mixed reality applications.

The developer ecosystem for Vision Pro is characterized by innovation and diversity. Developers are not only adapting existing apps for the mixed reality interface but are also creating entirely new experiences that leverage the unique capabilities of the device. This diversity of applications spans various domains, from healthcare and education to entertainment and productivity.

One of the kcy strengths of the developer ecosystem is the collaboration between Apple and developers to unlock the full potential of Vision Pro. This collaboration goes beyond providing tools and resources; it includes actively working with developers to explore new possibilities and overcome challenges in the mixed reality space. Apple's commitment to fostering a collaborative environment ensures that the platform evolves with input from a diverse range of creative minds.

The development tools provided for Vision Pro enable developers to harness the power of spatial computing, advanced sensors, and the immersive features of the device. From creating interactive educational experiences to designing innovative healthcare applications, developers have the tools to bring their visions to life in ways that were previously unimaginable.

The ecosystem is not just about individual developers; it's about a community that shares insights, best practices, and collectively pushes the boundaries of mixed reality. Developer forums, conferences, and collaborative initiatives contribute to a vibrant and dynamic ecosystem where ideas are exchanged, challenges are addressed, and innovation flourishes.

Moreover, Apple's commitment to user privacy and security is reflected in the guidelines and policies set for developers. This ensures that the mixed reality experiences created for Vision Pro adhere to high standards of privacy protection, fostering user trust in the platform.

CHAPTER SEVEN

The Launch and Beyond

February 2nd Release in the US

The anticipation surrounding the release of Apple Vision Pro reached its zenith as the mixed reality headset made its debut on February 2nd in the United States. This marked a significant milestone in the tech industry, as Apple stepped into the immersive world of mixed reality, promising a transformative experience for users.

The February 2nd release in the US was met with fervent excitement from

Apple enthusiasts, tech enthusiasts, and those eager to embrace the next frontier of personal computing. Apple's strategic choice of the release date underscored the company's commitment to making a grand entrance into the mixed reality landscape. The decision to launch on this specific date was likely driven by meticulous planning, aligning with marketing strategies and ensuring a smooth rollout of the device.

The release date wasn't just a formality; it was a moment that signaled a new era in personal computing. Apple Vision Pro wasn't merely a product; it represented a paradigm shift, a doorway to a mixed reality future that had been eagerly anticipated. The release in the US was the culmination of years of research, development, and innovation, showcasing Apple's dedication to pushing the boundaries of what's possible in technology.

International Release Plans

Following the February 2nd release in the US, Apple unveiled its plans for the international launch of Vision Pro, outlining a phased rollout that would bring the mixed reality headset to users across the globe. The international release plans signaled Apple's commitment to ensuring a global reach for its innovative product.

While the initial release in the US set the stage for the global introduction of Vision Pro, the subsequent international rollout was a carefully orchestrated expansion. Apple, known for its meticulous approach to product launches, likely considered factors such as market demand, logistical considerations, and regulatory approvals in different regions.

The international release plans generated considerable anticipation and speculation among tech enthusiasts worldwide. Apple's global footprint and its ability to create a seamless user experience across diverse markets heightened the expectations for a successful international rollout. Users outside the US eagerly awaited the opportunity to immerse themselves in the mixed reality experiences promised by Vision Pro.

The phased international release not only allowed Apple to manage logistics efficiently but also facilitated localized support and app adaptation. Different regions have unique user preferences, cultural nuances, and regulatory requirements, and Apple's approach to a gradual international rollout demonstrated a commitment to addressing these diverse factors.

Early User Experiences and Reviews

As Apple Vision Pro found its way into the hands of users, early experiences and reviews began to emerge, offering insights into the real-world impact of the mixed reality headset. Users, tech journalists, and early adopters shared their impressions, paving the way for a broader understanding of how Vision Pro was shaping up in the eyes of those who had the opportunity to explore its capabilities.

Early user experiences highlighted the transformative nature of mixed reality, with users expressing awe at the seamless integration of digital content into their physical surroundings. The spatial computing breakthrough, the immersive 3D experiences, and the innovative features like EyeSight technology and spatial audio garnered praise for their ability to redefine how users interacted with technology.

Reviews, both from tech experts and everyday users, contributed to a comprehensive understanding of

Vision Pro's strengths and areas for improvement. The comfort and customizable design of the headset were lauded, emphasizing the importance of user-centric design in the adoption of such groundbreaking technologies. The absence of lag, thanks to the M2 and R1 processors, received positive feedback, underlining the significance of responsive performance in mixed reality.

However, early reviews also shed light on considerations for future iterations. Some users expressed a desire for even more lightweight designs, extended battery life, and expanded compatibility with a broader range of applications. As with any pioneering technology, there were insights into the learning curve associated with embracing mixed reality, reinforcing the importance of intuitive user interfaces and educational resources.

The collective feedback from early users and reviews contributed to a dynamic feedback loop, offering Apple valuable insights for potential updates, enhancements, and refinements. The iterative nature of technology development allows for continuous improvement, and the early user experiences played a vital role in shaping the trajectory of Vision Pro beyond its initial launch.

In conclusion, the launch of Apple Vision Pro on February 2nd in the US marked a pivotal moment in the evolution of personal computing. The international release plans and subsequent early user experiences and reviews provided a holistic view of the device's impact, setting the stage for the continued evolution of mixed reality technology. As the global user base expanded, Vision Pro's journey moved beyond its launch, creating ripples of innovation, exploration, and user engagement in the ever-evolving landscape of mixed reality.

CHAPTER EIGHT

Technical Specifications: In-Depth Look at Hardware and Software

Apple Vision Pro's technical specifications represent a convergence of cutting-edge hardware and innovative software, creating a mixed reality powerhouse that promises to reshape the landscape of personal computing. The intricate interplay between the device's hardware and software components is the bedrock of its capabilities, offering users an immersive and seamless mixed reality experience.

Hardware Overview:

At the heart of Vision Pro's hardware is the dual-chip architecture, combining the M2 processor with the R1 processor. The M2 processor, known for its high-performance computing capabilities, handles general computing tasks, ensuring the smooth operation of applications. On the other hand, the R1 processor is dedicated specifically to mixed reality experiences, excelling in rendering 3D environments and managing spatial tracking. This collaboration between the M2 and R1 processors is the linchpin of Vision Pro's ability to eliminate lag and deliver a responsive mixed reality environment.

The advanced camera system, comprised of 12 cameras and LiDAR scanners, plays a pivotal role in spatial computing. The cameras capture a comprehensive view of the user's surroundings, enabling precise tracking of movements and gestures. LiDAR technology adds another layer of precision, creating a detailed real-time map of the environment. Together, these sensors ensure that the digital elements seamlessly align with the user's physical space, creating a cohesive and immersive mixed reality experience.

EyeSight technology is a standout feature, subtly revealing the user's eyes during operation. This not only enhances the realism of virtual interactions but also serves as a presence indicator, contributing to the social dynamics of mixed reality experiences.

The modular design of Vision Pro adds a layer of comfort and customization. Adjustable straps, adaptable components, and a focus on ergonomic considerations ensure that users can wear the device comfortably for extended periods. The lightweight and balanced construction contribute to an unobtrusive experience, allowing users to focus on the mixed reality content rather than the hardware.

Software Integration:

Vision Pro's software integration is a testament to Apple's prowess in creating seamless and intuitive user experiences. The device operates on a specialized mixed reality operating system that optimally utilizes the capabilities of the M2 and R1 processors. The operating system serves as the bridge between the hardware and the mixed reality applications, ensuring a fluid and responsive interaction.

The software environment is designed to seamlessly adapt familiar iOS and iPadOS apps to the Vision Pro interface. This adaptability extends the device's usability by providing instant access to a vast library of software in a mixed reality context. The infinite canvas for apps and 3D multitasking capabilities redefine how users engage with digital content, offering a spatial computing paradigm that transcends traditional interfaces.

Vision Pro's spatial computing breakthrough is underpinned by the software's ability to project information and applications directly onto the user's field of vision. This projection is dynamic, responding to the user's movements and gestures in real-time. The result is an immersive experience where digital elements seamlessly integrate into the physical world.

The integration of spatial audio into the software enriches the overall mixed reality experience. Whether in FaceTime calls, exploring virtual environments, or enjoying immersive entertainment, spatial audio creates an audio landscape that aligns with the spatial computing paradigm, enhancing realism and engagement.

Performance Metrics and Capabilities

Apple Vision Pro's technical specifications come to life through its performance metrics and capabilities, showcasing the device's prowess in delivering an unparalleled mixed reality experience. From lag elimination to spatial tracking precision, the performance metrics provide a comprehensive view of Vision Pro's capabilities across various dimensions.

Lag Elimination and Responsiveness:

One of the standout achievements of Vision Pro lies in its ability to virtually eliminate lag, delivering an experience that is not only seamless but also remarkably responsive. The dual-chip architecture, with the M2 and R1 processors working in tandem, ensures that general computing tasks and mixed reality rendering are handled with efficiency. This synergy between processors translates into real-time responsiveness, whether users are navigating through virtual environments, interacting with 3D content, or engaging in immersive experiences.

The absence of lag is a critical factor in preventing discomfort and disorientation often associated with virtual and augmented reality environments. Vision Pro's commitment to delivering a smooth and responsive experience sets a new standard in mixed reality devices, establishing it as a leader in the realm of personal computing.

Spatial Tracking Precision:

Spatial computing relies heavily on precise tracking of movements and gestures, and Vision Pro achieves this with remarkable accuracy through its advanced camera system and LiDAR scanners. The 12 cameras strategically positioned around the device capture a comprehensive view of the surroundings, allowing for accurate depth perception and understanding of the user's position in relation to digital content.

LiDAR technology, with its ability to create a detailed real-time map of the environment, further enhances the precision of spatial tracking. The combination of cameras and LiDAR scanners ensures that Vision Pro not only responds to large movements but captures subtle gestures, providing users with an intuitive and immersive mixed reality experience.

EyeSight Technology and Presence Indicator:

EyeSight technology, a unique feature of Vision Pro, serves as a presence indicator by subtly revealing the user's eyes. This technological feat adds a layer of authenticity to virtual interactions, contributing to the realism of social dynamics in mixed reality experiences. The presence indicator, facilitated by EyeSight technology, goes beyond technological innovation; it addresses a fundamental aspect of human communication by preserving eye contact in virtual interactions.

Spatial Audio Enhancement:

The integration of spatial audio into Vision Pro's capabilities enhances the overall realism and immersion of mixed reality experiences. Whether in FaceTime calls or exploring virtual environments, spatial audio creates a nuanced and three-dimensional audio landscape. This technology replicates the natural way we perceive sounds in the physical world, adding a layer of directionality to voices and creating an audio experience that aligns with the spatial computing paradigm.

Modular Design for Comfort:

The modular design, emphasizing comfort and customization, contributes to the overall user experience. Adjustable straps, adaptable components, and a focus on ergonomics ensure that users can wear Vision Pro comfortably for extended

CHAPTER NINE

Applications Across Industries

Healthcare

Apple Vision Pro's innovative mixed reality capabilities find profound applications in the healthcare industry, revolutionizing how medical professionals deliver care and how patients experience treatment. The convergence of advanced hardware and software in Vision Pro introduces a new dimension to healthcare, unlocking possibilities that were once confined to the realm of imagination.

One of the transformative applications in healthcare is in surgical training and planning. Vision Pro's spatial computing breakthrough allows surgeons to visualize intricate anatomical structures in 3D, providing a more comprehensive understanding of patient anatomy before entering the operating room. This immersive approach enhances surgical precision, reduces risks, and contributes to improved patient outcomes.

In patient care, Vision Pro facilitates remote consultations and telemedicine with an unprecedented level of immersion. Healthcare providers can virtually enter a patient's environment, examine symptoms, and collaborate with colleagues in real time. This not only enhances accessibility to medical expertise but also fosters a more personalized and engaging patient-doctor interaction.

Moreover, Vision Pro's advanced cameras and spatial tracking capabilities enable healthcare professionals to monitor patients in real time, even from a distance. This is particularly impactful for home-based care scenarios, chronic disease management, and post-operative recovery. The device's ability to seamlessly integrate into healthcare workflows positions it as a transformative tool for delivering patient-centered care.

Education

In the realm of education, Apple Vision Pro serves as a catalyst for transforming traditional learning models into immersive and interactive experiences. The device's spatial computing capabilities redefine how students engage with educational content, opening up new possibilities for understanding complex concepts and enhancing retention.

For subjects like anatomy or physics, Vision Pro brings educational content to life by allowing students to explore 3D models and simulations. Instead of studying flat images or diagrams, students can interact with virtual representations, gaining a deeper understanding of spatial relationships and structures. This hands-on approach fosters active learning and caters to various learning styles.

Collaborative learning takes center stage with Vision Pro, as students can work together in shared virtual spaces. Whether they are solving problems, conducting experiments, or exploring historical events, the device facilitates collaborative activities that transcend physical boundaries. This not only prepares students for a digitally connected world but also cultivates essential teamwork and communication skills.

Teachers can leverage Vision Pro to create engaging and dynamic lessons. By projecting educational content directly into students' field of vision, educators can guide them through immersive experiences that go beyond traditional classroom methods. The device's adaptability to familiar iOS and iPadOS apps ensures a seamless integration into existing educational ecosystems.

Entertainment

Apple Vision Pro reshapes the landscape of entertainment by immersing users in captivating and interactive experiences that transcend traditional forms of media consumption. The device's spatial computing breakthrough and advanced sensors create a new frontier for entertainment, blurring the lines between the physical and digital worlds.

In gaming, Vision Pro offers a level of immersion that goes beyond conventional gaming experiences. Users can navigate through virtual environments, interact with 3D characters, and experience gameplay in a way that feels tangible and lifelike. The spatial tracking capabilities ensure that movements are translated seamlessly into the virtual space, creating a gaming experience that transcends traditional boundaries.

Beyond gaming, Vision Pro transforms how users consume multimedia content. Whether it's watching movies, attending virtual concerts, or exploring interactive storytelling experiences, the device elevates entertainment to a new dimension. The life-size viewing experience and spatial audio create an immersive audio-visual journey that transcends the limitations of traditional screens.

Additionally, Vision Pro opens up possibilities for social entertainment. Users can connect with friends in shared virtual spaces, attend virtual events together, and experience entertainment in a collaborative and interactive manner. This social dimension of entertainment aligns with the growing trend of shared virtual experiences.

Business and Productivity

In the business and productivity landscape, Apple Vision Pro emerges as a transformative tool, enhancing collaboration, productivity, and the way professionals interact with digital content. The device's spatial computing capabilities and seamless integration of familiar applications redefine how business tasks are approached and executed.

One of the notable applications is in virtual meetings and collaboration. Vision Pro's FaceTime reinvention brings a sense of shared presence to video calls, making remote meetings feel more like in-person interactions. The life-size video tiles and spatial audio contribute to a realistic and engaging virtual meeting environment, fostering effective communication among team members.

Vision Pro's spatial computing breakthrough extends to the realm of data visualization and analytics. Professionals can interact with 3D models of complex data sets, gaining new insights and perspectives. Whether it's architectural designs, financial models, or scientific simulations, the device provides a dynamic platform for visualizing and analyzing information in an immersive manner.

The applications in business extend to training and skill development. Vision Pro's ability to simulate real-world scenarios allows professionals to undergo realistic training experiences. From honing technical skills to practicing presentations, the device provides a versatile platform for professional development.

Furthermore, the device's modular design ensures comfort during extended usage, making it well-suited for professionals who rely on digital interfaces throughout their workday. The customization options cater to individual preferences, allowing users to tailor the device to their unique needs.

In conclusion, Apple Vision Pro's applications across industries illustrate the device's versatility and transformative potential. Whether in healthcare, education, entertainment, or business and productivity, Vision Pro emerges as a catalyst for innovation, redefining how users engage with digital content and interact with the world around them. The spatial computing paradigm and advanced features create a multifaceted tool that goes beyond traditional computing devices, unlocking a new era of possibilities across diverse sectors.

CHAPTER TEN

Comparisons with Other MR Headsets

Assessing Competing Technologies

As the mixed reality (MR) landscape continues to evolve, various headsets have entered the market, each with its unique set of features and capabilities. Assessing competing technologies allows us to understand the positioning of Apple Vision Pro in the broader context of mixed reality headsets.

One key player in the MR space is Microsoft's HoloLens. HoloLens, known for its early entry into the market, focuses on augmented reality (AR) experiences. It overlays digital content onto the user's physical environment, making it suitable for applications like remote assistance, training, and visualization. While HoloLens excels in certain enterprise applications, its field of view and immersive capabilities may not match those of a dedicated MR headset like Apple Vision Pro.

Another notable contender is Meta Quest 2, a virtual reality (VR) headset that has gained popularity for its affordability and standalone capabilities. Unlike Apple Vision Pro, which prioritizes mixed reality, Meta

Quest 2 primarily offers virtual reality experiences. While it provides an immersive VR experience for gaming and entertainment, it doesn't bridge the physical and digital worlds in the same way as Vision Pro.

Magic Leap, another player in the mixed reality space, has garnered attention for its spatial computing technology. Magic Leap One overlays digital content onto the real world, similar to HoloLens. However, challenges with field of view and limited applications have impacted its widespread adoption.

When assessing competing technologies, factors such as field of view, spatial tracking precision, application ecosystem, and comfort play a crucial role. Apple Vision Pro distinguishes itself by offering a balanced blend of these elements, aiming to provide a comprehensive mixed reality experience.

Unique Selling Points of Apple Vision Pro

Apple Vision Pro stands out in the mixed reality landscape due to its unique selling points, which set it apart from other MR headsets. These distinct features contribute to the device's appeal and its potential to redefine personal computing.

Spatial Computing Breakthrough:

One of the standout features of Apple Vision Pro is its spatial computing breakthrough. Unlike some competing technologies that primarily focus on augmented or virtual reality, Vision Pro seamlessly blends the physical and digital worlds. By projecting information and applications directly onto the user's field of vision, it eliminates the confines of traditional screens and introduces a new dimension of interaction.

The spatial computing breakthrough is not just about visual immersion; it's about creating an intuitive and natural way to interact with digital content. The precision tracking facilitated by 12 cameras and LiDAR scanners allows for accurate spatial mapping, enabling digital elements to coexist harmoniously with the user's physical environment.

Dual-Chip Architecture: M2 and R1 Processors:

The dual-chip architecture featuring the M2 and R1 processors is a technological powerhouse that enhances the performance of Vision Pro. The M2 processor handles general computing tasks, ensuring the smooth operation of applications, while the R1 processor is dedicated specifically to mixed reality experiences. This collaboration eliminates lag, offering a responsive and immersive mixed reality environment.

Competing headsets may lack the dedicated mixed reality processor found in Vision Pro, affecting their ability to seamlessly integrate digital content into the user's surroundings. The dual-chip architecture positions Vision Pro as a device designed from the ground up for mixed reality, providing a level of performance and responsiveness that sets it apart.

EyeSight Technology and Presence Indicator:

EyeSight technology, with its ability to subtly reveal the user's eyes, serves as a unique feature in Vision Pro. This goes beyond mere technological innovation; it becomes a presence indicator that adds a layer of authenticity to virtual interactions. In comparison, many other headsets may lack such nuanced features that contribute to the social dynamics of mixed reality experiences.

The presence indicator not only enhances realism but also addresses a fundamental aspect of human communication—eye contact. In virtual interactions, where physical presence is simulated, the ability to convey the direction of one's gaze adds a layer of human connection that goes beyond visual and auditory aspects.

Seamless Integration of iOS and iPadOS Apps:

Apple Vision Pro leverages the strength of Apple's ecosystem by seamlessly integrating familiar iOS and iPadOS apps into its mixed reality interface. This integration ensures that users have instant access to a vast library of software, offering a familiar and user-friendly experience. Other MR headsets may not benefit from such an established and diverse app ecosystem, limiting their versatility and usability.

The ability of Vision Pro to adapt existing apps to the mixed reality interface contributes to its accessibility and ease of use. Users can leverage the functionality of apps they already know, making the transition to mixed reality more intuitive and reducing the learning curve associated with new technologies.

Modular Design for Comfort and Customization:

The modular design of Vision Pro prioritizes user comfort and customization. Adjustable straps, adaptable components, and a focus on ergonomics ensure that users can wear the device comfortably for extended periods. This focus on comfort sets Vision Pro apart, as extended use is often a concern in the adoption of immersive technologies.

Competing headsets may not offer the same level of comfort and customization, potentially limiting their suitability for prolonged use. Vision Pro's commitment to user-centric design extends beyond just technological innovation, addressing the physical comfort of users and enhancing the overall mixed reality experience.

In conclusion, Apple Vision Pro's unique selling points, including its spatial computing breakthrough, dual-chip architecture, EyeSight technology, seamless app integration, and modular design, position it as a frontrunner in the mixed reality landscape. These features not only set it apart from other MR headsets but also contribute to its potential to redefine personal computing and user experiences in a mixed reality future.

CHAPTER ELEVEN

Looking Ahead: Future Updates and Features

As Apple Vision Pro makes its debut, the anticipation for future updates and features is palpable. Apple's commitment to innovation and iterative development suggests that Vision Pro is poised to evolve, offering users a glimpse into the exciting possibilities that lie ahead.

Iterative Enhancements:

Apple's track record with its products, including iPhones, iPads, and Macs, demonstrates a commitment to continuous improvement through iterative updates. Similarly, Vision Pro is likely to receive regular software updates that introduce new features, enhance performance, and address user feedback. These iterative enhancements will contribute to refining the user experience and expanding the capabilities of the mixed reality headset.

The dual-chip architecture of Vision Pro, featuring the M2 and R1 processors, provides a robust foundation for future improvements. As Apple continues to push the boundaries of its chip technology, users can expect performance boosts, enabling even more complex and immersive mixed reality experiences.

Expanded App Ecosystem:

The integration of iOS and iPadOS apps into Vision Pro is a compelling aspect that is likely to see further expansion. As developers embrace mixed reality and create unique experiences for Vision Pro, the app ecosystem is poised to grow. This growth will not only bring a wider range of applications but also foster creativity and innovation in how users interact with digital content in mixed reality.

Future updates may introduce tools and resources that empower developers to create even more immersive and specialized applications for Vision Pro. This could lead to a diverse ecosystem of mixed reality apps spanning various industries, from education and healthcare to entertainment and business.

Enhanced Spatial Computing:

Spatial computing is at the core of Vision Pro's unique capabilities, and future updates may further refine and expand this aspect. Improved spatial tracking precision, advancements in gesture recognition, and enhancements to the seamless blending of digital and physical worlds are areas where Apple may focus its attention.

The sophistication of the camera system and LiDAR scanners in Vision Pro provides a solid foundation for spatial computing improvements. Users can anticipate more precise and nuanced interactions in mixed reality scenarios, making the device even more intuitive and immersive.

Collaborative and Social Features:

As mixed reality becomes more ingrained in our daily lives, collaborative and social features are likely to take center stage in future updates. Apple may introduce tools that enable enhanced collaboration in virtual spaces, making Vision Pro a compelling platform for remote work, education, and social interactions.

Features like shared virtual environments, collaborative

workspaces, and expanded social experiences could become integral parts of Vision Pro's capabilities. This would align with broader trends in technology, where connectivity and shared experiences play crucial roles in shaping user interactions.

Innovations in Hardware Design:

Apple is renowned for its commitment to design innovation, and future updates to Vision Pro may include advancements in hardware design. The modular design, which already prioritizes comfort and customization, could see further refinements. This may include advancements in materials, additional customization options, and improvements to the overall ergonomics of the device.

As technology evolves, Apple might explore ways to make Vision Pro even more lightweight and compact, ensuring that users can enjoy extended mixed reality experiences without physical strain. Additionally, innovations in display technology could contribute to enhanced visuals, further immersing users in the mixed reality environment.

Anticipated Developments in the MR Landscape

As Apple Vision Pro paves the way for mixed reality adoption, the broader mixed reality (MR) landscape is expected to witness significant developments. These developments, driven by technological advancements, industry trends, and user preferences, will shape the future of MR experiences beyond Vision Pro.

Interoperability and Standardization:

One anticipated development in the MR landscape is increased interoperability and standardization. As mixed reality devices from various manufacturers enter the market, there is a growing need for standardized protocols that enable seamless communication between different devices. This would pave the way for a more interconnected mixed reality ecosystem, allowing users with different MR headsets to collaborate and share experiences.

Standardization efforts could extend to software frameworks and development tools, streamlining the creation of mixed reality applications that are compatible across a range of devices. This would benefit developers by reducing fragmentation and expanding the reach of their applications to a broader audience.

Integration with AI and Machine Learning:

The integration of artificial intelligence (AI) and machine learning (ML) is expected to play a pivotal role in advancing the capabilities of mixed reality. AI algorithms can enhance object recognition, gesture tracking, and even contribute to more intelligent and context-aware virtual assistants within mixed reality environments.

Anticipated developments include improved AI-driven interactions, where mixed reality devices understand user intent more intuitively. Whether it's anticipating user gestures or providing contextually relevant information, the marriage of AI and mixed reality is poised to create more personalized and intelligent user experiences.

Advancements in Haptic Feedback:

Haptic feedback, which provides a sense of touch in virtual environments, is an area that is likely to see significant advancements. Future MR devices may incorporate more sophisticated haptic feedback mechanisms, allowing users to feel textures, pressure, and even simulate resistance in the virtual world.

This development could greatly enhance the realism and immersion of mixed reality experiences, making virtual interactions more tangible. For example, in a healthcare simulation, a medical professional using mixed reality could feel the resistance when interacting with virtual anatomical structures, creating a more lifelike and training-rich environment.

Wider Adoption in Professional Industries:

As mixed reality matures, there is an anticipated increase in its adoption across professional industries. Beyond gaming and entertainment, mixed reality is expected to become an integral tool in fields such as architecture, engineering, healthcare, and education. Professionals in these industries may rely on MR devices for design visualization, surgical planning, virtual training, and collaborative workspaces.

The success of devices like Apple Vision Pro in addressing specific industry needs could catalyze broader adoption, driving the development of industry-specific applications and workflows. This, in turn, could lead to a more

Conclusion

Summing Up the Vision Pro Experience

As we bring our exploration of Apple Vision Pro to a close, it's essential to encapsulate the immersive journey this mixed reality headset promises. Vision Pro is not merely a device; it's a portal into a new dimension of personal computing that seamlessly blends the physical and digital worlds. The amalgamation of cutting-edge hardware, innovative software, and a commitment to user-centric design culminates in an experience that transcends traditional computing paradigms.

The spatial computing breakthrough achieved by Vision Pro represents a pivotal moment in the evolution of personal technology. No longer confined to flat screens, users step into a world where digital content dances around them in three dimensions. The projection of information directly onto the field of vision, powered by the dual-chip architecture of the M2 and R1 processors, eliminates lag and ensures a level of responsiveness that redefines our expectations.

The twelve cameras and LiDAR scanners intricately woven into Vision Pro's design form a sophisticated system that tracks movements and gestures with meticulous precision. Navigating and interacting with the digital realm becomes an intuitive extension of one's physical actions. The modular design, with its emphasis on comfort and customization, ensures that users can immerse themselves in this new reality for extended periods without sacrificing comfort.

Apps are not confined to rectangular windows or limited desktops; Vision Pro opens up an infinite canvas where users can arrange and interact with applications in 3D space. The integration of familiar iOS and iPadOS apps seamlessly adapts them to the mixed reality interface, providing instant access to a vast library of software in a novel light.

Memories are transformed into vivid spatial experiences, capturing moments in stunning 3D. Whether reliving memories or exploring existing photo and video libraries at a life-size scale, Vision Pro offers a level of realism and immersion that redefines how we interact with our personal media.

Connection deepens with FaceTime reinvented. Life-size video tiles of loved ones float in virtual space, creating a sense of shared presence. Spatial audio adds another layer of realism, making voices seem to originate from their respective positions in the virtual space, fostering immersive and intimate connections.

Beyond these features lie the unique aspects that set Vision Pro apart. EyeSight technology subtly reveals the user's eyes, providing a presence indicator that enhances virtual interactions. The modular design ensures a comfortable and customizable fit, making the device adaptable for a wide range of users. A growing ecosystem of developers is crafting unique experiences tailored specifically for Vision Pro, pushing the boundaries of what is possible in mixed reality.

The Impact on Personal and Professional Computing

The launch of Apple Vision Pro signifies a monumental shift in both personal and professional computing. This mixed reality headset is not just a gadget; it's a doorway to a future where the boundaries between the physical and digital worlds blur, creating an entirely new way of interacting with technology.

Personal Computing Redefined:

For personal computing, Vision Pro marks a departure from the familiar screens and interfaces we've grown accustomed to. It introduces a spatial computing paradigm that places digital content seamlessly into our physical environment. The impact is not just visual; it's experiential. Users find themselves immersed in a world where applications, memories, and connections take on a three-dimensional form.

The device's ability to transform memories into spatial experiences adds an emotional layer to personal computing. Whether reliving a cherished moment or exploring a library of memories, Vision Pro creates a bridge between the digital and the sentimental. It's not just about viewing photos; it's about stepping into them.

The spatial computing breakthrough also redefines how users engage with applications. No longer confined to flat surfaces, apps become dynamic elements that users can arrange and interact with in three-dimensional space. The integration of familiar iOS and iPadOS apps ensures that users can seamlessly transition into this new computing paradigm without sacrificing the functionality they're accustomed to.

Connection takes on a new dimension with FaceTime reinvented. Virtual meetings become lifelike gatherings where loved ones are present in a shared space. Spatial audio enhances the sense of presence, making virtual interactions more natural and engaging. EyeSight technology adds a touch of humanity by revealing the user's eyes, creating a subtle yet impactful indicator of presence in virtual conversations.

Professional Computing Transformed:

In the realm of professional computing, Vision Pro emerges as a transformative tool that goes beyond conventional devices. The impact is felt across various industries, redefining how professionals collaborate, innovate, and engage with digital content.

Healthcare professionals find a powerful ally in Vision Pro, using its spatial computing capabilities for surgical planning, remote consultations, and patient monitoring. The immersive nature of the device enhances training and skill development, offering realistic simulations that bridge the gap between theory and practice.

Education undergoes a revolution as Vision Pro becomes a catalyst for interactive and immersive learning experiences. Students step into three-dimensional worlds, exploring subjects like never before. The device fosters collaborative learning, preparing students for a digitally connected world where teamwork and communication are paramount.

In the business landscape, Vision Pro introduces a new dimension to virtual meetings and collaboration. Professionals engage in lifelike meetings, where the spatial computing breakthrough brings a sense of shared presence. The device becomes a versatile tool for data visualization, design collaboration, and realistic training scenarios.

Beyond these applications, Vision Pro's impact extends to industries such as entertainment, where gaming experiences become more immersive, and virtual events take on a new level of engagement. The device's modular design ensures comfort during extended use, making it a practical tool for professionals who rely on digital interfaces throughout their workday.

As we conclude our exploration of Apple Vision Pro, it's evident that this mixed reality headset is not just a product launch; it's a groundbreaking step into the future of computing. Vision Pro unleashes a new dimension where the physical and digital worlds seamlessly coexist, offering an immersive experience that transcends traditional computing boundaries.

The spatial computing breakthrough, powered by the dual-chip architecture and supported by a sophisticated camera system and LiDAR scanners, creates a mixed reality experience that is unparalleled in its responsiveness and precision. Vision Pro redefines how we interact with digital content, breaking free from the limitations of flat screens and introducing a dynamic canvas for apps, memories, and connections.

The impact on personal computing is profound, as Vision Pro transforms the way we engage with our memories, applications, and connections. It goes beyond visual immersion, touching the sentimental with the ability to turn memories into spatial experiences. The reinvention of FaceTime and the subtle indicator of presence through EyeSight technology add a layer of humanity to virtual interactions.

In the professional landscape, Vision Pro becomes a transformative tool across diverse industries. From healthcare and education to business and entertainment, the device reshapes how professionals collaborate, innovate, and engage with digital content. Its modular design ensures comfort during extended use, making it a practical and versatile tool for a wide range of applications.

Apple Vision Pro is more than just a headset; it's a portal to a future where the possibilities of computing are limitless. As the device makes its debut, the anticipation for future updates, developments in the mixed reality landscape, and the ongoing impact on personal and professional computing sets the stage for a journey into uncharted territories. Vision Pro is not just a glimpse into the future; it's the unleashing of a future where the boundaries between the physical and digital worlds fade away, opening up new dimensions of experience, interaction, and connection.

www.ingramcontent.com/pod-product-compliance
Lightning Source LLC
Chambersburg PA
CBHW060105260726
48658CB00004B/1412